# EATING THE VEGETARIAN WAY

BY THE SAME AUTHOR

America Goes to the Fair,
*All About State and County Fairs in the USA*

East Africa, *Kenya, Tanzania, Uganda*

Egypt, *Rebirth on the Nile*

Ethiopia, *Land of the Lion*

Ghana and Ivory Coast, *Spotlight on West Africa*

The Global Food Shortage,
*Food Scarcity on Our Planet and What We Can Do About It*

Mexico, *Crucible of the Americas*

Puerto Rico, *Island Between Two Worlds*

# EATING THE VEGETARIAN WAY

## GOOD FOOD FROM THE EARTH

### by Lila Perl

illustrated with photographs

WILLIAM MORROW AND COMPANY/NEW YORK/1980

Library of Congress Cataloging in Publication Data

Perl, Lila.
  Eating the vegetarian way.
  Includes index.
  Summary: Discusses the reasons for vegetarianism, the different types of vegetarian diets, and why modern meat-raising techniques are causing many Americans to change their diets. Also offers alternative protein rich recipes.
  1. Vegetarianism—Juvenile literature.   2. Vegetarian cookery—Juvenile literature.   3. Nutrition—Juvenile literature.   [1. Vegetarianism.   2. Vegetarian cookery.   3. Nutrition]   I. Title.
TX392.P45   613.2′62   80-18416
ISBN 0-688-22248-X   ISBN 0-688-32248-4 (lib. bdg.)

Permission for use of photographs is gratefully acknowledged to the following: New York Public Library Picture Collection, pages 21, 25; United Nations, pages 14, 15, 18, 26, 30, 32, 34, 36, 37, 47, 53, 54, 72, 73, with special credit to Cida/White, pages 41, 68; A. Holcombe, page 43; H. K. Lall, page 40; Ray Witlin, pages 20, 64; Wheat Flour Institute, page 67. All other photographs are by the author.

**DESIGN BY PATRICIA LOWY**

# CONTENTS

# RECIPE CONTENTS

# EATING THE VEGETARIAN WAY

# CHAPTER ONE

# ALL KINDS OF VEGETARIANS

At this very moment, somewhere in the world, people are sitting down to dinner. What are they eating?

In a West African village, families are gathered around pots of peppery vegetable stew thickened with ground peanuts. Into the stew they dip balls of *fufu*, a thick, pasty mash made from a starchy root or tuber such as cassava or yam. They then deftly bring *fufu*, stew juices, and vegetables to their mouths. Across the world in a Mexican adobe hut, freshly baked, pancakelike tortillas made from ground corn serve as handy scoops for cooked beans spiced with dried chili peppers. On yet another continent, a sari-clad Indian woman sets out dishes of rice, lentils, and stewed eggplant hotly flavored with curry, India's favorite seasoning.

Nobody seems to be having a bit of meat for dinner.

Some Americans, accustomed to bacon for breakfast, a hamburger for lunch, and steak for dinner, may find this menu rather surprising. But, in fact, most people in the world eat little meat or none at all. They live on corn, rice, wheat, barley, or other grains, fresh vegetables, dried peas and beans (also called "legumes" or "pulses"), nuts, and other foods that spring directly from the earth. In other words, they are vegetarians all or most of the time.

About fourteen million years ago, all of us were vegetarians. The advanced ape that was our ancestor and lived mainly in the trees probably ate some insects, but otherwise he was strictly a herbivore, an eater of plant foods.

Eventually this prehuman creature descended from the

*Above:* Tortillas, the pancakelike "bread" of Mexico and Central America
*Opposite:* Preparing a meal of rice and lentils in an Indian home

trees and learned to live on the ground, walking upright on two legs. He was on his way to developing into an ape-man and was acquiring hunting skills. By about four million B.C., he had begun to kill small animals for his food, using rocks, thick tree limbs, or whatever other natural weapons lay about. In any case, he was becoming an omnivore, that is, a meat eater, or carnivore, as well as a plant eater.

Although our bodies have changed in hundreds of ways

from the time of preman, we all bear a telltale sign of our one-time vegetarianism—our appendix.

This shrunken, leftover organ is a dangling pouch that extends from a section of our large intestine. A wormlike three inches on the average, it has no function in our present digestive system. But in a much earlier stage of our development, the appendix was longer and thicker, and it provided an important storage area for the woody stalks, chewy leaves, tough barks, and hard seeds that our plant-eating ancestors consumed. Like one of the four chambers of a cow's stomach, the appendix held those coarse fibers until the rest of the digestive system could get around to breaking them down into nutritious substances.

Today, of course, food of that kind would be totally indigestible for us. Even the roughage in apples, grains, and celery passes through our bodies undigested. As for our appendix, we seldom think about it unless it gives us trouble, becoming infected and inflamed through accidental contact with the bacteria in the large intestine. Then it often must be removed by surgery.

Further evidence of our vegetarian past is the diet of our distant cousins, the great apes. Gorillas and chimpanzees are still primarily plant eaters, munching on fruits, vines, leaves, buds, barks, blossoms, and seeds. Like preman, apes and monkeys also eat ants, termites, beetles, and other insects.

Recent studies of *some* groups of African chimpanzees living in the wild have revealed that they do occasionally kill and eat small or baby animals. It has also been found that gorillas living in zoos will sometimes eat meat. Perhaps these species, too, are in the very early stages of becoming omnivores. After all, evolution is still going on, and none of us can assume that human beings *or* apes are in their final stage of development.

*    *    *

Though man has become fully capable of eating meat and could not survive in places like the polar regions unless he ate an almost completely carnivorous diet of caribou, seal, walrus, and other meats, there have always been people in meat-eating societies who clung to a vegetarian diet.

One of the first vegetarians of record is the Greek mathematician and philosopher Pythagoras, who lived during the sixth century B.C. Known primarily for an important theorem concerning the geometry of the triangle, he is also called the "father of vegetarianism," a man who pleaded with his followers to eat only the "innocent" foods of the earth, such as apples, grapes, grains, herbs, vegetables, and honey.

One of the reasons Pythagoras opposed the slaughter and consumption of animals was that he believed the human soul was immortal and moved into a new body after death, perhaps that of an animal. While it might be necessary, Pythagoras admitted, to kill a wild beast in self-defense, it was still wrong to eat it. Besides, he pointed out, the domesticated animals eaten by man, such as cattle and sheep, were not themselves beasts that killed for food. They lived peacefully on grass.

The ideas of Pythagoras about the transmigration of souls—their ability to pass from one body to another—were shared by many early religious groups. He may even have drawn his ideas from his travels in the East, where he probably came in contact with the Hindu religion of India. Although Hindus had once customarily sacrificed and eaten cattle, by the sixth century B.C., they were beginning to come under the influence of a reformist religious sect known as Jainism.

So deep is the Jainist reverence for all forms of life that to this day Jains will not eat potatoes, radishes, carrots, turnips, or other root vegetables because by uprooting them a worm may be deprived of its food or an insect dislodged from the soil. Some very devout followers of Jainism wear nose and mouth coverings to avoid breathing in tiny organisms or microscopic forms of life, and they refuse to wear any garments made of feathers, fur, wool, leather, or even silk.

Many of the taboos, or forbidden practices, of the Jains are reflected in modern Hinduism, the religion of most of the people of India. Among the animals that are sacred to the Hindu is the cow, which symbolizes man's link with all life, especially animal life. Thus, the cow may not be slaughtered

A sacred cow wanders through the marketplace in a village in India.

in much of India, and beef must never be eaten by religious Hindus. Even a road accident in which a wandering cow is injured can lead to violence. Often an angry crowd gathers and demands punishment for the driver and passengers of the automobile.

Although they are revered, the sacred cows of India are scrawny, often diseased creatures, their ribs showing beneath their thin, sagging flanks. Usually they amble listlessly through mud-brick villages, along country roads and main highways, and even through the streets of big cities. Sometimes a cow that meanders into a farmer's field to munch on the sprouting crops will be driven off, but it will never be harmed.

Foreigners find it difficult to understand how this waste of meat can be permitted where so many people are ill-nourished and hungry. But Hindus do not give way to butchering cattle even in the worst periods of famine. They do, however, use cow dung, which they dry for cooking fuel, and some Hindus drink cow's urine, believing in its purifying properties.

Many Hindus exclude not only beef but all other kinds of meat from their diet as well. Hindu vegetarians may drink milk, but they avoid eating eggs, for consuming the embryo of an unborn chick is another way of taking life.

One of India's most famous vegetarians was Mohandas K. Gandhi, who tried to show that a meatless diet and a non-violent way of life were closely related. During Gandhi's youth, in the late 1800's, India was under British rule. Many young Hindus turned to meat eating at that time because they believed that a meat-heavy diet gave the English their tall stature. In contrast, most Indians were short and slight.

A popular jingle of the day went:

> *Behold the mighty Englishman—*
> *He rules the Indian small,*
> *Because being a meat eater*
> *He is five cubits tall.*

Indian farmers dry cow dung, which is used
to fertilize fields and as cooking fuel.

As a cubit is about eighteen inches, this measure would
make the Englishman an exaggerated seven and a half feet tall.

Gandhi, who never grew over five feet, five inches, was
tempted to try goat meat for the first time at the age of thir-
teen. He later regretted it, saying that he felt "as though a

Mohandas K. Gandhi as a youth of fourteen, a year after
his much-regretted experience of eating animal flesh

live goat were bleating inside me." In his later years, as the leader of the Indian independence movement, he became a strict vegetarian, not even drinking milk, and went on many long fasts when he drank nothing but water.

Only a few religions, like Hinduism, have decreed a vegetarian way of life, but some, like the Jewish religion, have set up rules about the method of slaughtering animals. Under the laws of Judaism, slaughterers must cut the animal's neck as swiftly and as painlessly as they can, and they must drain away as much of the animal's blood as possible.

Meat and milk products may not be eaten together because the Torah, the earliest book of Hebrew law, says, "Thou shalt not seethe a kid in its mother's milk." Jews are also not permitted to eat an egg with a blood spot in it, because the spot shows that the egg has been fertilized and that a new life has begun to form.

Certain kinds of meat and fish are taboo to religious Jews—pork and shellfish, such as shrimp, oysters, and lobsters. (Pork is also forbidden to Muslims, the followers of Islam.) Because these creatures scavenge among dead and rotted matter for their food, they are considered unclean. As insects are also prohibited, orthodox Jews must be very careful not to bite into a wormy apple or other fruit.

If a group of famous past vegetarians assembled at some meatless banquet in the great beyond, the odd assortment of guests would be astounding. At one end of the table might be Leonardo da Vinci, the great fifteenth-century Italian artist, painter of the "Mona Lisa." At the other end might sit Adolf Hitler, the dictator who led Germany into the Second World War and was responsible for the extermination of six million Jews.

To understand da Vinci's reasons for abstaining from meat, we need only look at his magnificent drawings of all forms of life—detailed, accurate, and yet deeply caring. Although, like all artists of his day, he learned human and animal anatomy by dissecting corpses, he believed that human beings should not live by inflicting death on cattle, sheep, goats, and other food animals. He wrote, "He who does not value life does not deserve it."

Hitler was a different kind of vegetarian. It is hard to believe that a man who deliberately put millions of human beings to death could have cared deeply about the lives of animals. Possibly his earliest refusals to eat meat, in meat-eating Austria and Germany, were acts of rebellion that sprang from the rejection and anger he experienced in his teens. Hitler was also a hypochondriac, overcome with worries about his health, and seems to have blamed meat for the stomach upsets he experienced. Perhaps he feared that he would be contaminated by some disease passed on by a butchered cow or pig.

In any case, Hitler's vegetarianism was one of the worst diets in history. Even as a youth he had a sweet tooth that could not be satisfied, and he seldom ate the grains and vegetables that are the standbys of the meatless diet. When he could afford them, he indulged in rich, creamy cakes and desserts. When he was too poor to buy the whipped-cream confections of the Vienna pastry shops, he cooked rice for himself and smothered it with sugar.

Another outstanding vegetarian who would certainly have to be present at the banquet is George Bernard Shaw, the Irish-born British dramatist who died in 1950 at the age of 94. Although Shaw did not approve of hunting as a sport, he was not especially concerned about the killing of animals, particularly those that were destructive, poisonous, or nuisances. His main objection to meat eating was the "unnecessary waste of the labor of masses of mankind in the nurture and slaughter of cattle, poultry, and fish for human food."

Shaw also considered meat unhygienic and admitted to a

personal distaste for animal flesh. Boasting about his healthy appearance in his later years as compared with that of meat eaters, he said, "What can you expect from people who eat corpses?"

Witty, sometimes to the point of rudeness, Shaw probably enjoyed being different and even carried around personal menus to be distributed to the kitchen staffs of hotels and steamships when he traveled.

In the 1800's, the United States produced its own home-grown vegetarians. Most of us have eaten Graham crackers, but few may know that they are named for Sylvester Graham, a New Jersey minister who lived from 1794 to 1851. Graham was a social reformer and health advocate who opposed hard drinking, heavy meat eating, and the greasy, overcooked foods popular with most Americans. He believed in a vegetarian diet of natural foods, especially whole wheat rather than white flour.

Graham breads, cakes, and cookies came about through his efforts to put the nourishing bran and germ that were part of the whole-wheat berry back into flour. There were even Grahamite boardinghouses, which served healthful vegetarian meals and no beer, wine, or liquor.

Graham's mission was followed in the mid-1800's by the birth of a new American religious sect—the Seventh Day Adventists. Although Christians, the Adventists adopted Saturday as their Sabbath (as in Judaism). On that holy day followers were required not to work. In addition, one of the sect's founders, Ellen White, taught that the body was God's temple and must not receive the flesh of God's creatures.

Besides the practice of vegetarianism, she urged Adventists to avoid pastries and other rich desserts and to abstain from tobacco and alcohol. Today there are about 500,000 Seventh Day Adventists in the United States.

In a sense, both Sylvester Graham and Ellen White were

Sylvester Graham, the New Jersey minister
who tried to reform the American diet

nineteenth-century inaugurators of the health-food movement that has taken hold so strongly in the United States today. They were among the first to try to alter the American meat-eating tradition that had sprung from the game-rich frontier. But these two reformers did not merely call for an end to eating meat; they proposed a diet that accented natural plant foods such as whole grains and fresh vegetables, foods that offered good nutrition in themselves.

In this slaughterhouse, the entrails and organs on the table have been cut from the carcasses hanging in the background.

Over the centuries there have been all kinds of vegetarians and all sorts of reasons for choosing a meatless diet. Some of these reasons can be seen in the choices that many young people are making nowadays as they turn to vegetarianism.

The young child who loves animals may have difficulty coming to terms with the idea of meat eating. Other young people may simply experience disgust and revulsion at the sight of dead fish, bloody meats, or limp, butchered chickens.

Teen-agers sometimes choose to be vegetarians to assert their individuality or their independence. Others may be idealists; helpless and frustrated, they embrace vegetarianism as a means of taking a stand against injustice.

In addition, there are sound nutritional and strong economic reasons for a meatless diet. The world is full of people who are vegetarians not by choice but by necessity. Meat is expensive—costly to produce, costly to purchase—and there is simply not enough to go around. A very wide gap separates the world's rich meat eaters from its involuntary vegetarians.

To help us understand why only a privileged minority can afford to eat a meat-rich diet while many have not enough plant food to subsist on, we need to explore further and find out exactly what is needed to raise meat animals in today's crowded, land-scarce world.

# CHAPTER TWO

# THE QUEST FOR PROTEIN

Picture a warm summer's evening. In backyards all across the United States the smoke of charcoal fires is rising, and soon the familiar odor of charring meat wafts on the breeze. Down at the local hamburger chain business is brisk. Double, jumbo, and monster-size burgers, enclosed in puffy white rolls, quickly vanish into waiting mouths. The hot dog drive-in is crammed with customers too. So is the fried-chicken place, even though chicken is only half as popular as red meat.

Americans have been having a love affair with steaks, hamburgers, and hot dogs for a long time now; meat is their favorite source of protein. A typical company dinner or restaurant meal is steak, baked potato, and apple pie. The average fast-food meal is a hamburger, french fries, a Coke or a shake.

What is protein and why is it so important in the human diet? Protein is a vital nutrient that is converted into the substances from which most of our body tissues—bones, blood, skin, muscles, internal organs, enzymes—are made. We need some protein in our meals every day to replace cast-off cells and to rebuild, maintain, and regulate our bodies.

Meat, poultry, fish, eggs, milk, and cheese are all rich sources of protein. Although meat from wild and domesticated animals always figured in the American diet, our grandparents and great grandparents ate much less of it than we do today. They consumed only half to two-thirds as much beef, and chicken was a special dish reserved for Sunday dinner. Milk and cheese were also less popular foods in the early 1900's. Breads and cereals, root vegetables, dried beans and peas, and

Harvesting wheat, a plentiful crop in the United States and Canada

other protein-rich plant foods made up a larger share of the total food intake than they do now.

Today the beef cattle that supply our most popular national food have become the sacred cows of America. Unlike the sacred cows of India, they are raised strictly for slaughter and, with the help of special feeds, drugs, and other chemicals, are made to grow heavy and fat as rapidly as possible.

The cost of raising cattle is very high. A calf that begins life at 100 pounds must weigh around 1000 pounds at slaughtering time a little over a year later, and more than half of this weight is made up of the bones, hide, and other inedible parts. To produce such growth, enormous amounts of cattle feed are required. The fodder includes tons of wild pasture grasses, forage (specially grown animal-feed crops like alfalfa and clover), and crops that are also grown to feed human populations, such as corn, sorghum, wheat, millet, soybeans, and other grains and legumes. A great deal of fertile farmland, scarce in many parts of the world, is needed to grow all these crops.

Beef cattle, hogs, sheep, goats, chickens, and other domesticated meat animals are really "machines" for converting plant foods into meat and other animal-protein products like milk and eggs. As Ellen White, the Seventh Day Adventist leader, wrote, "Those who eat flesh are but eating grains and vegetables at second hand, for the animal receives from these things the nutrition that produced growth."

Unfortunately, large meat animals are not very efficient converters of plant foods into flesh. Those that are fattened on grains, as in the United States, western Europe, Russia, and Japan, are both inefficient and the most expensive to raise. For example, eight to ten pounds of grain are needed to produce just one pound of beef.

Why do some countries feed grain to their cattle, while others, like Argentina, New Zealand, and Australia, let their animals roam the grassy pasturelands and eat their fill? Once upon a time cattle were raised on wild grasses in the United States, too. But by the late 1800's, as farming expanded into the Great Plains, the rangelands began to shrink. For a while, the ranchers and the farmers of the Old West were at logger-

Argentine cattle feed on grassy
pasturelands rather than farm-grown crops.

heads, but they soon came to terms, for the cereal crops the farmers were growing turned out to be even more nourishing feed than the field grasses that had been plowed under.

The cost of the new feed was not that much greater either, for the United States was rich in grain production. All through the twentieth century, until the early 1970's, there seemed plenty to go around: enough for fattening meat animals, enough for American tables, and even a surplus which could be given away to starving peoples in famine-struck areas.

American cattlemen also discovered more economical ways to meet the growing demand for beef. Animals that roamed less and ate more got fatter faster, so they developed something called the "feedlot," where cattle could be fattened for the kill. Today thousands of beef animals spend the last four to six months of their lives crowded together in pens, unable to walk about freely, eating the grains and legumes that will finish them for market. In meat-packing language, *finishing* means fattening that not only adds to the animal's weight but produces well marbled steaks and chops—meat with lots of fat distributed throughout the lean muscle fibers, which are the real source of protein.

Americans have learned to like their meat this way; it is much more tender and juicy than the meat of cattle that have toughened their muscles by moving about the range. In countries that have little or no rangeland, such as the small, crowded islands of Japan, cattle are kept in pens almost all the time and are given especially grown feeds throughout their lives. This beef is the most expensive in the world.

American and other grain-finished beef has become expensive too. In the early 1970's, prices suddenly took an enormous jump. This increase was brought about by several factors, mainly the growing demand of prosperous peoples all over the world for grain-fed beef and by widespread crop failures in Africa, Asia, and Russia.

Opposite: In this feedlot, cattle are crowded
into pens to be fattened for slaughter.

Because there simply was not enough grain to feed people
and animals, many people in the poorer countries starved to
death during the emergency. If grains are consumed in *direct*
form—as wheat, corn, rice, or sorghum (the four most widely
eaten grains in the world today)—they can feed a great many
people. But if they are eaten in *indirect* form, as the flesh of
cattle, hogs, or poultry, they can feed only a relative few.

Americans, who eat about 30 percent of all the animal
products in the world (even though the United States has less
than 6 percent of the Earth's population), consume about
2000 pounds of grain per person each year, most of it indirectly
in the form of beef, pork, and chicken. Meantime, people who
are too poor to have a high-meat diet live on only 500 pounds
a year of rice, corn, or other grains. Eating plant foods directly
from the earth is known as eating low on the food chain. Meat
eaters, on the other hand, eat high on the food chain, a practice that global agricultural experts consider wasteful of our
planet's resources.

Where does the nutritive value go when grains, legumes,
and other plant foods move up the food chain? Much is ex-
pended for energy as the animal moves about; much is excreted
as waste matter; the rest is converted into hide, hair, hooves,
bones, blood, organs, and muscle. However, the only parts of
the animal that serve as food are the muscle and a few of the
organs, mainly the liver.

How much beef, pork, lamb, veal, chicken, and turkey do
Americans eat each year? About 230 pounds per person, approximately 95 pounds of which is beef, 65 pork, and 50
chicken. How much meat do the world's vegetarians by necessity eat? As little as 2 pounds a year, and seldom more than 7
or 8. Clearly the wealthy, meat-eating societies are hogging

Severe drought and a world grain shortage caused starvation
in the Sahel, the area south of the Sahara Desert, in the early 1970's.

the world's meat supply as well as its grain supply and, therefore, most of the protein.

Meanwhile, people of poorer societies must try hard not
only to get enough to eat, but to get enough protein to main-

tain health. Too little protein in the diets of children is especially dangerous because their bodies are growing rapidly. People in Asia, Africa, South America, and the West Indies know all too well the symptoms of kwashiorkor. This protein-deficiency disease shows up in infants who have been weaned

Eating low on the food chain: Indian schoolgirls
have a lunch of rice and vegetable pancakes.

from protein-rich mother's milk and put on a diet of thin, starchy gruel made from a staple food such as cassava, plantain (cooking bananas), corn, sorghum, or rice. These foods are what most of the adults in those societies eat. The baby's stomach swells, its arms and legs grow puffy with water accumulation, its skin becomes blotchy and scaly, and its hair turns pale reddish or blond. The death rate among these "red babies" is high, and those that do survive usually suffer stunted growth and may be mentally retarded.

A combination of certain plant foods *can* provide protein of good quality, but if even plant foods are scarce, the tendency of the world's hungry and malnourished people is to search out less popular forms of animal protein.

Hamburger-eating Americans may wince, but many Africans welcome a meal of roasted locusts or termites, and some Mexicans enjoy crisp, fried maguey worms, picked from the maguey cactus plant that grows over much of Mexico. In many parts of the world, flying insects like butterflies and moths may be snapped up on the wing and swallowed as a between-meals snack, while carefully collected sun-dried ants, crickets, and grasshoppers are pounded into a flour. Insects, abundant everywhere, make good food because they are high in protein and are a source of vitamins and minerals as well. Our apelike ancestors must have known instinctively about the benefits of insects in the diet.

Small wild animals, from rodents to monkeys, go into the stewpot in many countries. In Ghana and other parts of West Africa a large field rat, about the size of a rabbit, is prized for its meat and the gravy it makes. Along Ghanaian country roads freshly killed grasscutters, as the rats are locally known, are offered for sale to passing motorists. In South America rodents like the guinea pig and the white-fleshed agouti have long been used for food, and in jungle Mexico the meat of spider monkeys is smoked like pork and grilled over hot coals.

The ancient Romans ate grilled songbirds, thrushes, larks, sparrows, and nightingales; the Indians of the Americas rounded up dogs, which they fattened for the cooking pot; the frontiersmen and settlers of the southern United States put the meat of squirrels, a member of the rodent family, into their famous Brunswick Stew. These animals are still being eaten today.

Even cannibalism has been practiced as a means of survival or to improve an impoverished diet. A glance into the American past calls to mind the "starving time" of 1609-1610 in Jamestown, Virginia, and the ill-fated Donner party, snowbound in the Sierra Madre Mountains of California, in 1846. In both instances, survivors ate their dead companions. In Jamestown, one man was accused of having pickled and eaten his wife. In modern times, the survivors of an airplane crash in the snowy, desolate Andes of South America stayed alive by cannibalizing the bodies of others who had died.

Sometimes cannibalism is practiced as part of a religious ritual; it is believed that the admirable traits of the eaten will pass into the eater. For this reason, the Aztec priests of Mexico may have drunk the blood and eaten the hearts and limbs of the brave warriors chosen to be sacrificed to the god of war. On the other hand, some historians think that the Aztecs may have killed and eaten people because of the scarcity of game in their area. In the case of certain Polynesian peoples, they seem simply to have developed a liking for human flesh, which they called "long pig."

Although the animals eaten by people of other cultures may seem peculiar, repulsive, or downright barbaric to us, they are, in any case, cheap. Insects, birds, and wild animals do not have to be fed expensive grains or other edible plants that could be used for human food.

Certain domesticated animals do serve a useful purpose in poorer cultures because they graze land too arid, steep, or

Sheep in Afghanistan are raised on dry,
rugged land that is not suitable for farming.

rocky to be farmed. Goats and sheep can convert coarse grasses
and spiky shrubs into meat and milk for human consumption.
Middle Eastern herders and village dwellers from Turkey to
Afghanistan, who eat the meat of these animals, do not expect
the tenderness of grain-fed beef, and they also utilize the
heart, liver, kidneys, brains, and other nourishing animal
organs. The eyeballs, a special delicacy, are so highly prized
that they are reserved for honored guests.

Surprisingly, some animal-herding peoples like the nomadic Tuareg of North Africa's Sahara and the Masai of East Africa eat meat only occasionally. The Tuareg keep numbers of camels as beasts of burden and milking animals, and they also graze sheep and goats. However, they prefer to hunt down a desert gazelle or antelope for the cooking pot and keep their

A Tuareg: These nomads keep camels and other herding animals for milk but seldom slaughter them for meat.

herds intact. Animals that provide milk, butter, and cheese represent wealth on the hoof and are a sign of prosperity. Besides, livestock is essential for buying a bride as it is an important feature of the bride price, or "bridewealth." The Masai herders, too, seldom slaughter their cattle and instead live primarily on a mixture of milk and blood drawn from the neck veins of their animals.

The sea is a wide-ranging source of protein. Japanese and Mediterranean peoples have long eaten varieties of fish unfamiliar to many Americans—wriggly-armed squid and octopus, black-shelled mussels, spiny sea urchins, and excessively bony or odd-tasting sea creatures known commercially as trash fish. The Japanese also learned early in their history that seaweed, first used as fertilizer, can be a valuable, mineral-rich food.

Some of the peculiar-seeming foods in the Chinese diet may have resulted from the desperate search for sustenance during the famines that repeatedly swept that land. The population learned to eat dried flowers such as tiger lilies, the roots of swamp-growing lotus plants, birds' nests, fermented buried eggs, and other unusual foods that have become part of the Chinese cuisine.

When the peoples of the Orient did have bits of meat or fish, they stretched them with rice or noodles and vegetables. In addition, they learned from early on to use soybeans, probably the earth's best single source of plant protein, in their diet.

In addition to soybeans, there are many other kinds of dried beans and peas that are good sources of protein, especially when they are combined with grains. In the Far East, India, Mexico, and Central and South America, where little animal protein is available to most people, legumes have long been popular. But in the United States, people eat only about six pounds of dried beans per person per year.

A modern-day market in Shanghai, featuring
some of the many plant foods in the Chinese cuisine

Little by little, all of us are beginning to realize that flesh can feed only a few while plant foods—beans, grains, vegetables, fruits, nuts, and seeds—can feed many and feed them well. Some people in our society, after looking at the global scene, have actually become vegetarians in protest against the meat-heavy American diet and the way in which it monopolizes world food resources.

Others among us may begin to think of eating less meat for more selfish reasons. Meat is the costliest item on the American menu, and eating less of it can save money. Meat is also high in fat and often in chemical content, and many people consider it a serious health threat. It has been medically linked to obesity, heart disease, and cancer. So, for a variety of reasons—mainly conscience, cost, and health—even the staunchest of American meat eaters may soon find themselves taking a closer look at vegetarianism.

# CHAPTER THREE

# THE NEW VEGETARIANISM

Lunchtime is approaching, your stomach has been rumbling for the past hour, and your mouth is watering for a fast-food hamburger meal—bun, pickles, ketchup, french fries, a chocolate shake—the works.

Lots of people say that fast food is poor nutrition, but after all a hamburger is meat, and everyone knows that meat is an excellent source of protein.

True, but would you believe that you could get just as much or more protein if you had a peanut-butter sandwich on whole-wheat bread and a glass of milk or a cup of yogurt instead of that burger lunch? You would do better because the standard fast-food hamburger provides practically the only protein in that meal, about 13 grams. The rest is fat (in both the meat and the french fries), salt, starch, sugar, and additives, especially the gums, emulsifiers, and artificial flavorings used to make the milkless chocolate shake thick, foamy, and chocolate-tasting.

The peanut-butter-sandwich lunch, on the other hand, is better nutrition all around. It is packed with protein, at least 22 grams. At the same time, it has only about 440 calories compared with 780 calories in the hamburger meal. You could add a piece of fresh fruit (about 100 calories) and drizzle a tablespoon of honey or jelly on your peanut-butter sandwich (about 60 calories), and still there would be no more than 600 calories in the meal.

These facts about the hamburger lunch may seem confusing because we have always been told that meat is special because of its protein content. In fact, meat and other animal products —poultry, fish, eggs, cheese, and milk—*are* special in the sense that they contain protein in a ready-to-use form that our bodies find very convenient.

If we take a closer look at protein, we see that it is made up of chemicals called "amino acids." The human body needs about 22 different amino acids, most of which it can make out of any sort of protein, from animal or plant foods. But there are 8 special, or essential, amino acids that the body cannot manufacture. They must come in a complete, properly balanced set from the food we eat. Meat and other animal products have all 8, which is why they are known as complete proteins.

Vegetables have proteins too, yet vegetables usually play supporting roles at best. The reason protein-rich vegetable foods like dried peas and beans, grains, nuts, and seeds are shoved onto the sidelines is that they do not have all eight essential amino acids in the right proportions. So they are known as incomplete proteins.

Incomplete, though, does not have to mean inadequate. Take the example of the beans and the corn tortillas of the Mexicans and Central Americans, or the lentils and rice of India. Beans, lentils, and other legumes tend to be low in the essential amino acid, methionine, but high in the amino acid, lysine. Corn, rice, wheat, and other grains are low in lysine, but high in methionine. Yet when the two are put together, they have the same high-protein nourishment found in meat or eggs.

Foods that form complete proteins when they are combined are known as complementary proteins. Combining them simply means eating them in the same meal, not hours

*Opposite:* A Guatemalan woman grinds corn for tortillas, which are almost always eaten with beans for high-protein nourishment.

apart, so that they can be broken down in the digestive tract together. Fortunately, there are a great many complementary-protein combinations that can be made with plant foods. Peoples in various parts of the world have been living on such combinations since biblical times at least, when the diet in and around the Holy Land consisted mainly of barley or other grains along with chick-peas (also known as garbanzos) or lentils.

Kidney, lima, navy, pink, black, brown, and pinto, or spotted, beans are just a few of the other varieties of dried peas and beans that can be successfully combined with grains. In the Far East the soybean, a high-quality plant protein because of its nearly perfect amino-acid balance, has been eaten for close to 5000 years.

In the Orient soybeans often turn up not as cooked beans but as soy "cheese," which is made from the curd of soy "milk" (soybeans cooked in water). This healthful Chinese and Japanese specialty, which goes by the general name of tofu, consists of pale, bland-tasting cheeselike blocks, firm or slightly shivery. Tofu has many uses in soups, salads, vegetable dishes, sauces, dressings, and desserts, and it gives top-quality protein value when it is eaten with rice, wheat, or other grains. Nowadays this ancient Chinese food is beginning to be better known in the United States.

Indonesians have an even tastier kind of soybean cake, known as tempeh, made from fermented hulled-and-soaked beans. There is also a dark-colored fermented soybean paste known as miso, well-liked by the Japanese. Soy sauce, with which almost all of us are familiar, originated as the runoff of miso and has a similarly sharp, salty flavor.

Although the United States today grows most of the world's soybeans, a large portion of the crop is fed to livestock and nearly all the rest is either exported to Japan and other nations for human food or pressed into oil. In general, Americans

find the taste of cooked soybeans unappealing and complain
that they are hard to digest as well.

The Mexicans and the people of India, with their grain-
and-legume diets, are not the only groups that have lived successfully as vegetarians for generations, even though they never
knew anything about amino acids or *why* their food patterns
worked. North Africans have long eaten a coarse-grained porridge known as couscous, made from cracked wheat (called

Soup made with barley and chick-peas, a complete-protein
combination that goes back to biblical times

"bulgur") or from millet or sorghum. They combine this cereal with a vegetable stew—often spiced with red pepper, ginger, mint, or curry seasoning—that always contains chick-peas. People of the Caribbean and South America have favored dishes like pigeon peas, black beans, or other legumes with rice ever since the Spanish conquerors brought rice to the New World in the sixteenth century.

Today this new understanding of how incomplete plant proteins complement each other to make up complete proteins is often referred to as "the new vegetarianism." Because modern science has enabled us to break down and examine the composition of foods, we have learned about other combinations that work, such as dried beans and sesame seeds, peanuts and sunflower seeds, and grains and soy products. We even know how to balance the strengths and weaknesses of three or four different plant foods and combine them for all sorts of high-protein breakfasts, snacks, soups, main dishes, breads, cookies, and desserts. Thus, the protein in a meal can be spread over several courses. It does not have to be concentrated, for example, in one huge, expensive steak that brings with it a great deal of fat and consequently, a great many calories.

In other words, vegetarians—those who never eat a bit of meat and avoid all other animal products, including milk, cheese, and eggs—simply have different ways of making up the eight essential amino acids, just as a dollar can be made up of two half dollars, four quarters, ten dimes, twenty nickels, a hundred pennies, or any combination of these coins. As long as the coins add up to one hundred, they are just as good as the crispest, newest dollar bill.

All along we have been talking, of course, about strict vegetarians, people who eat nothing *but* plant foods. They are also known as vegans. Most vegetarians, however, have a broader range of foods to choose from, for they also eat dairy products like milk, skim milk, buttermilk, yogurt, cream, butter, and cheese. They are known as lacto-vegetarians.

Lacto-vegetarians consider dairy products acceptable because they do not involve the killing of animals. The single exception is cheese, which is customarily made with rennet extract, a curdling agent that comes from the lining of the fourth stomach of a milk-fed calf. To obtain the enzyme rennin from which the extract is made, the animal must be slaughtered. But there are rennetless cheeses and cheeses curdled with vegetable extracts, which lacto-vegetarians can find in health-food stores. Also available are kosher cheeses that conform to Jewish dietary laws prohibiting the mixing of meat and milk products.

When plant foods such as grains are combined with dairy

Pizzas, one example of the many valuable lacto-vegetarian combinations

products (which are already complete proteins), the protein quality of the grain soars. The reason is that milk, yogurt, and cheese are especially high in lysine, the amino acid in which rice, wheat, and corn are low.

Peanuts, low in lysine though they belong to the lysine-rich legume family, also combine well with milk. If a grain like whole-wheat bread is present too, the amino-acid patterns improve even more, which explains the high protein value of the peanut-butter-sandwich lunch that includes milk or yogurt. Because milk products can make up for other amino-acid deficiencies in legumes, beans provide complete protein when they are eaten with cheese, for example.

Potatoes are still another plant food that combines well with dairy products. Although potatoes have a small amount of protein, it is of very high quality because of its excellent amino-acid balance. Their complete protein is greatly increased in potato soups, puddings, pancakes, and casseroles made or served with milk or cheese. And many other lacto-vegetarian dishes are high in protein too. Macaroni and cheese, pizza, rice pudding, even a simple cheese sandwich, are just a few examples.

Nomadic herding peoples have always traded some of their milk and other dairy products for grains grown by settled farmers. Thus, dishes that make use of both foods are often found in their cultures. The Tuareg of the Sahara combine camel's milk, goat's milk, or goat cheese with couscous. They also make a nourishing combination of fresh camel's milk and their own oasis-grown dates. The milk has the protein while the dates have iron, an important mineral that is low in milk. In addition, dates provide fiber, or roughage, also absent in milk, which is considered beneficial to the passage of waste material through the human digestive tract.

Some of the healthiest and most long-lived peoples in the world, like the inhabitants of the Hunza region on the north-

Arab women bake bread on large iron "griddles."

ern Pakistan slopes of the Himalayas and the Soviet Georgians of the Caucasus mountains, are lacto-vegetarians, living mainly on grains and fermented milk products such as yogurt. The Hunza people bake their whole-wheat flour into chapattis, individual pancakelike rounds of bread. Although the Himalayan terrain and climate are too harsh for raising dairy cows, the Hunzas keep domesticated yaks, shaggy, long-haired oxen, which provide rich milk and butter. The goats they raise yield both milk and cheese. The Hunzas never studied nutrition, but with remarkable intuition they long ago began to cultivate apricot trees during the short mountain summers and to include the iron-rich dried fruit, as well as many kinds of nuts, seeds, and legumes, in their milk-and-grain diet.

Yaks, used as beasts of burden in the snowy Himalayas, provide milk and butter for the farmers of the lower slopes.

In addition to vegans and lacto-vegetarians, there are also vegetarians who eat eggs. If they eat dairy products as well, they are known as ovo-lacto-vegetarians. Vegetarians vary on the question of including eggs in their diet because some feel that eating the embryo of an unborn chick or other bird is the same as taking a life. This belief would be true, however, only if the hen's egg had been fertilized by the rooster and was on its way to hatching into a baby chick.

Some ovo-vegetarians actually prefer fertile eggs, usually available in health-food stores, because they believe the rooster's hormones have made these eggs more nourishing. While the male hormones are vital to the unborn chick, so far there is no scientific proof that they play a part in human nutrition.

Whether fertilized or not, eggs are considered the perfect protein food—better than meat, milk, or cheese—because their amino-acid pattern is ideally balanced for maximum utilization by our bodies. Eggs are the standard against which the amino-acid patterns of all other protein-containing foods are measured. Including eggs in the vegetarian diet is a guarantee of excellent protein nutrition as well as a means of getting more variety by adding omelets, soufflés, crepes, custards, many kinds of baked goods, even a simple egg-salad sandwich.

Lacto-, ovo-, and ovo-lacto-vegetarians who take care to eat a well-balanced plant-food diet seem to get as sufficient an amount of proteins, vitamins, and minerals as meat eaters. Studies of Seventh Day Adventist groups have shown, in fact, that these vegetarians are even better off. Their diets contain more fiber and more of the healthful vegetable oils and complex carbohydrates (starches found in grains and legumes), than the average meat-eater's diet, which is often high in the less-nutritious animal fats and in sugars, or simple carbohydrates.

What about the vegan diet, which includes plant foods

only? Since strict vegetarians get adequate protein by combining plant foods with different amino-acid patterns, the only element that seems to be lacking in their diet is a single vitamin, $B_{12}$, which is found almost exclusively in animal products. A vitamin $B_{12}$ deficiency can lead to nervous disorders and to a certain type of anemia, so some vegans take a supplement in capsule form or in $B_{12}$-fortified yeast or soy milk. Others feel that they get enough of this vitamin from fermented soybean products and from seaweed, which are said to contain small amounts of $B_{12}$.

Real dangers crop up, however, when vegans try to limit the plant foods they eat. Those vegetarians called "fruitarians," for example, may actually try to live on a diet of fruits only. Fruits lack protein, and most lack calcium, a very important mineral. Also, except for avocados, they are too low in fat to support human health. Most fruitarians add nuts and seeds for some protein and fat. However, as the proteins are un-complemented and, therefore, incomplete, even this diet is usually inadequate.

Adding leafy greens and other raw vegetables, including sprouted grains and legumes (like alfalfa, wheat berry, and bean sprouts) helps a little more, especially with minerals and vitamins. But as most fruitarians believe in eating raw foods only, just as people did before the discovery of fire, they seldom include those protein-rich grains and legumes that require cooking. One of the problems with getting good nutrition from a raw-plant-food diet is that uncooked fruits and vegetables contain a great deal of water and fibrous bulk in proportion to their nutrients, and nuts and seeds contain a lot of fat in proportion to their protein value.

Another extremist vegetarian diet is the so-called brown-rice diet. Most of the people who have tried to live on it were followers of a man named George Ohsawa. Ohsawa, a Japanese who was born in 1893 and died in 1966, was the founder of the

The main items in a fruitarian, or raw food, diet; grains like the wheat kernels in the background would have to be sprouted to be eaten raw.

macrobiotic diet. Though sometimes called the "Zen macrobiotic," it is not really related to the Eastern religion of Zen Buddhism.

Ohsawa taught that some foods were yin, or feminine, and some were yang, or masculine. By balancing yin and yang foods through a series of ten increasingly limited diets, macrobiotic followers would at last attain the "highest" diet, which consisted of nothing but brown rice, perhaps a sprinkling of salt and sesame seeds, and a little green tea. This regimen was supposed to produce spiritual enlightenment, a goal of Ohsawa's program.

During the 1960's many young people were caught up in macrobiotics, which means "great way of life." However, the brown-rice diet violates so many principles of good nutrition that those who stayed on it for months became severely mal-nourished. Some grew so ill that they died. For them, the "great way of life" became a way of death.

These examples of bad vegetarian diets may raise the question of whether any vegetarian actually gets enough protein. Let's take a look at exactly how much the human body needs, figured in grams. A gram is .035 ounces, so 28 grams equal one ounce.

The World Health Organization (WHO), an agency of the United Nations, says that an adult woman needs 29 grams of protein a day, or about one ounce, and an adult man needs 37 grams. In the United States, the generally accepted figures are set by the Food and Nutrition Board of the National Academy of Sciences—National Research Council, although its *Recommended Daily Dietary Allowances* of protein, vitamins, and minerals are higher than those of WHO and other nutrition authorities.

For example, the NAS-NRC recommends between 44 and 56 grams of protein a day for adults (still no more than two ounces), and 23 to 34 grams for children aged one to ten. Between the ages of eleven and fourteen the requirement is 45 to 46 grams; between fifteen and eighteen, it is 46 grams for females and 56 for males.

Yet Americans eat an average of 90 to 100 grams of protein a day! Most of that protein comes from the beef, pork, and chicken that Americans feature in their meals as well as eggs, milk, and cheese. Often they add protein to protein in their favorite dishes, packing even more in—milk in the meat loaf, egg in the pork-chop or fried-fish breading, cheese on the hamburger.

Is there anything wrong with eating two or three times the amount of protein actually needed each day? Yes, there are some drawbacks. For one thing, it costs more. Animal proteins, especially meats, are very expensive. For another thing, excess protein is a waste. Those extra 40 or 50 grams eaten today cannot be stored in the body for future use as a tissue-building substance. Whatever protein the body cannot use each day is broken down and disposed of. By the following day, some has been burned as energy, some may have been stored as fat, and the rest has passed out of the body, mainly in the urine. Another disadvantage of eating extra protein is that the breakdown of large amounts can put an added strain on some of the body's organs such as the kidneys.

Eating a well-balanced diet the vegetarian way guarantees plenty of protein for bodily needs, but not a wasteful excess. And complementary plant proteins provide the same quality protein as meat. We can eat one and a third cups of rice and a half cup of dried peas or beans combined in a zesty Latin-American dish and they will equal the protein of a six-ounce steak. As far as the amino-acid content is concerned, the human body cannot tell the difference.

There *are* other differences, though, between a black-bean stew served with rice and a broiled steak, and the body *can* detect them. Surprisingly, the well-marbled steak may be far less healthful, not only because of its high fat content, but because of the growth hormones, antibiotics, and other drugs fed to beef cattle in the United States today that turn up as residues in the meat supply.

In an effort to sell more to more people and reap ever-higher profits, the giant American food industry has tampered with many of the items in our diet so that, by the time they come to market, a number of foods are no longer very nutritious. Vegetarians, and others who want full nutritional value from the foods they eat, are challenging the quality of the American food supply and demanding, above all, that it be wholesome and natural.

# CHAPTER FOUR

# EATING WHAT COMES NATURALLY

Suppose you decide to try being a vegetarian for a while. To make your new diet simple for the rest of the family, you plan to eat everything they eat for dinner except the meat course. In addition, you may substitute an egg or a cup of yogurt for the steak, chicken, hamburger, or meat loaf that provides the protein in your family's typical meal.

What's wrong with the remaining foods on the menu? They include a fruit cup of canned fruit cocktail, frozen french-fried potatoes, canned green beans, a salad of iceberg lettuce with bottled French dressing, a buttered white roll, and a dessert of store bought apple pie.

All of these typical American foods have one thing in common. Except for the iceberg lettuce, they are a long way from their natural state. Even the lettuce, which is grown on huge corporation-owned farms in California and Arizona and marketed by the same companies (called agribusinesses), is one of the least nutritious salad greens. It has less vitamin A, vitamin C, calcium, and iron than romaine lettuce or other varieties of leafy salad greens. But it is a favorite of the nation's major produce growers because it is most resistant to bruising and wilting and can be kept in cold storage for long periods of time. Finding more iceberg lettuce than any other kind at the supermarket, most Americans have unthinkingly accepted it as *their* favorite.

The rest of our typical American meal is made up of mass-produced, processed foods—foods that have undergone changes in freshness, flavor, texture, and food value as a result of such processes as refining, milling, canning, freezing, and other procedures.

Take the canned fruit cocktail and the apples in the apple pie. Both have been sweetened with refined white sugar, which nutritionists say supplies only "empty calories." A simple carbohydrate, sugar contains no vitamins, minerals, or protein, but adds 113 calories for every ounce swallowed.

Too much sugar in our diets causes tooth decay and overweight, and it can worsen serious illnesses such as diabetes. Yet Americans consume an average of 100 pounds of refined sugar a year, most of it in processed foods such as sodas and other soft drinks, presweetened breakfast cereals, desserts, canned and frozen fruits, jams and jellies, candy, chewing gum, and even in toothpastes, cough medicines, and vitamin capsules.

Most sugar enters our diets through processed foods.

Saccharin, a popular artificial sweetener that has no calories, often is substituted for sugar in soda pop and other foods in waistline-conscious America. Yet, in addition to being a potentially dangerous chemical that has been proved to cause bladder cancer in laboratory rats, saccharin does not seem to have cured America's sweet tooth. In fact, saccharin's sweetness seems to increase the craving for a rich dessert along with the diet soda or chemically sweetened coffee. Having saved the calories in the beverage, the would-be dieter often feels that the sugar-laden dessert is somehow "earned."

Unlike sugar-addicted Americans, there are still many rural peoples in Africa and other parts of the world who do not include any refined sugar in their diets. While most people naturally like the taste of sweet things, an almost boundless craving for sweets seems to be a learned response. Often it begins early in life when children are offered cookies, candy, and desserts as rewards or consolations. In less-developed societies, children are likely to chew contentedly on a stick of raw sugarcane straight from the fields. In this form the sugar is not very concentrated and has some vitamins and minerals that are lost in the refining. In addition, the fibers of the chewed cane are so tough and bristly that they clean the teeth better than a toothbrush.

As to the french-fried potatoes in the typical American meal, they simply add to a diet already too high in fat. Fats make up 42 percent of the total number of calories Americans consume. More fattening than proteins or carbohydrates, a gram of fat has nine calories against the four calories per gram of each of the other two nutrients. Doctors and nutritionists say that eating excess fat not only tends to cause obesity but may bring on heart attacks and other life-threatening diseases. The low rate of heart disease in Japan is believed to be related to the rice-fish-and-vegetable diet of most of the inhabitants. Only about 20 percent of their total calories come from fat.

A child in an Indian farming village chews raw sugarcane.

Frying potatoes in deep fat not only adds loads of calories, it destroys some of the nutrients (including most of the vitamin C) in this high-quality vegetable food. While a medium-sized baked potato has only about 100 calories, french fries and potato chips are so high in fat that about nine of them add up to 100 calories. And eating only nine potato chips is almost as hard as eating one salted peanut.

Even foods that don't ooze fat or make our fingertips greasy can be high in fat. Examples are processed foods like cake and pie-crust mixes, store-bought baked goods, crackers, fast-food shakes, imitation whipped cream and imitation coffee creamers, as well as all those salted snacks—corn chips, popcorn, cheese curls—that Americans pop into their mouths with the sugary sodas they drink.

Another item that Americans are getting far too much of is salt. Excess salt can lead to high blood pressure, a cause of strokes. In a stroke, parts of the brain are affected, causing paralysis, crippling, and even death.

Salty-tasting foods such as french fries, potato chips, pretzels, pickles, mustard, ketchup, and olives are easy to spot. But other processed foods like canned soups and gravies, canned and frozen vegetables, frozen dinners, and even many sweet-flavored processed foods contain a great deal of salt too. Fresh green beans, cooked crisply tender and lightly seasoned, would have more nutrients and much less salt than the canned beans served in our typical American dinner.

That roll made from white flour on our dinner menu is another example of a processed food that has lost much of its natural goodness. Kernels of wheat and other grains (which are really seeds) are made up of a white, starchy portion called the "endosperm," an outer husk that in wheat is called the "bran," and a third part called the "germ," which gives life to the new plant. When farming first began, approximately 7000 years ago, millers ground up the entire kernel of wheat,

Some of the many processed foods
that add too much salt to the American diet

barley, or other grains for bread flour and cereal porridge.

The presence of the bran and the germ in the flour made the bread coarse-textured, dark, and chewy. From very early times, millers began trying to isolate the endosperm so that the flour would be as smooth and white as possible. Until the development of modern flour-milling machinery only the rich could afford to eat fancy white bread and rolls and delicate sweet cakes. The poor went right on eating bread made with coarse whole-wheat flour.

Nowadays foods made with white flour are common for rich and poor in the United States and other wealthy industrial societies. At the same time we have begun to realize how much we have lost by eliminating the vitamin-, mineral-, and fiber-rich bran and germ of the wheat kernel. So, by Government regulation, flour manufacturers add three synthetic B vitamins and the mineral iron to white flour to put back the lost nourishment.

This process is called enrichment. However, about twenty-two nutrients, including the important protein in the wheat germ, are lost when flour is ground only from the endosperm. Therefore, enriched flour is still not as nourishing as whole-wheat flour. Thus, whole-wheat flour is strongly favored by vegetarians and others who seek the natural food value found in less-processed foods.

The same principle holds true for other grains. Brown,

Whole-wheat bread includes the germ and the bran of the wheat kernel.

or unpolished, rice has more vitamins, minerals, proteins, and fiber than white, or polished, rice. Those peoples who eat polished rice and little else tend to be more poorly nourished than those who eat brown rice as their staple.

Whole-grain cereals such as oatmeal and shredded wheat have the most food value. However, "instant" oatmeal and other instant-cooking cereals as well as the many puffed, flaked, and toasted dry cereals on the market are so highly processed that their nutritive value has been reduced.

Emaciated Africans of the Sahelian zone,
who live on polished grains and little else

Most pasta products like spaghetti, macaroni, and noodles are made with enriched white flour, but an even better choice for the health-conscious is the kind of pasta made with whole-wheat flour, usually found in health-food and other specialty stores.

Many of today's vegetarians question the healthfulness and wholesomeness of the plant foods in their diet because of the chemical fertilizers added to the soil in which they are grown and the strong chemical sprays—pesticides and herbicides—used to kill insect pests and curb weed growth. The residues of these chemicals found in food may well be health hazards. Foods such as dried peas, beans, lentils, and nuts are quite protected against plant sprays because they grow inside a pod or shell. But in the case of fruits, vegetables, and grains, vegetarians often favor those that are organically grown, raised without artificial fertilizers or chemical sprays.

Ideally, organically grown foods are a good idea, but in practice using natural animal manures for fertilizing, and controlling weeds and pests by natural methods, works best in home vegetable gardens or on small farms. Commercial food growers are unwilling to risk giant crop losses due to insect invasions. Moreover, several of the largest agribusinesses in the United States are also the manufacturers of pesticides and other widely used plant chemicals.

Although fresh meat might appear to be a natural food, the chemicals used in raising American beef cattle and other livestock have convinced some people, who are not vegetarians, that they should stop eating meat and poultry. Others have given up fish as well because of the industrial chemical wastes that now pollute many streams, lakes, bays, and other fishing grounds.

Beef cattle get an especially large dose of chemicals during their relatively short lifetimes. For one thing, they eat large quantities of forage and grains that have been sprayed with pesticides and herbicides while they were being grown. During their four- to six-month confinement in feedlots, the cattle stand shoulder to shoulder in their own manure, so they are given antibiotics to prevent disease and tranquilizers to reduce the stress that results from being crowded into such tight quarters.

Residues of all these chemicals show up to some degree in meat products. The antibiotics are similar to those given to human beings, and consumption of them may build up drug-resistant bacteria in the body. They may also cause allergic reactions in some people. Probably the most dangerous residue, however, is that resulting from the female growth hormone, diethylstilbestrol, popularly known as DES. DES has been fed to cattle in the United States since the 1950's. It increases the weight gain of the animals by 10 percent or more, saving cattlemen some of the cost of feed and allowing them to bring larger and heavier animals to market in record time.

DES is known to cause cancer in human beings. Pregnant women who took this drug in the early 1950's to prevent miscarriage gave birth to daughters who, some twenty years later, were found to have a rare form of cancer of the vagina.

The United States Government banned the use of DES in 1973 because of high residue levels found in beef muscle and especially in beef liver and kidneys. The ban was overturned in 1974, however, and the drug is still in use. No one knows for sure how much DES is in the beef Americans eat today, nor do they know what a safe residue level might be, for cancers caused by DES can take fifteen years or longer to develop.

Processed meats pose another problem. Once upon a time, meats were preserved by being soaked in brine, a strong salt solution, with lots of spices, or were slow-dried over smoke until they were hard and moisture-free. But today's frankfurters, bologna, salami, ham, bacon, corned beef, and other cured-meat specialties, as well as smoked fish, contain a chemical preservative called "sodium nitrite" and sometimes a simi-lar substance called "sodium nitrate." Nitrites and nitrates, in addition to being preservatives, act as coloring and flavoring agents in processed meats. In the human stomach, these chemi-cals can be converted into substances known as nitrosamines, which have been proved to cause cancer in laboratory animals and may do so in human beings as well.

About two-thirds of the 65 pounds of pork Americans eat each year is in processed form. Besides containing sodium ni-trite, hot dogs, bologna, bacon, and other processed meats are also high in salt and fat. The frankfurter you had for lunch could have been as much as 30 percent fat, and your breakfast bacon was probably at least 75 percent fat. Even the fast-food chicken you were planning to have for dinner is 50 percent fat, mainly in the coating.

Chemical residues are found in most of the chicken we eat, including the kind we prepare at home. Like today's feedlot cattle, American poultry is now raised assembly-line style. From the time of their birth the chicks are confined to indoor cages, arranged row upon row, several birds to a cage. Lights are kept on nearly around the clock to simulate endless day-light. Because crowding tends to cause disease and so much stress that some chickens become cannibalistic, poultrymen add both antibiotics and tranquilizers to the chickens' feed. They also spray the birds with pesticides against ticks and lice.

Fortunately, the practice of implanting DES pellets in the necks of chickens, which began in 1947, has been discontinued. It was banned in 1959, when a male restaurant worker who ate a great many chicken necks began to develop female character-istics, due to the high level of the hormone concentrated in the pellet-implanted necks. Can we be sure, however, that the chemical residues that do turn up in the chickens we now eat are entirely harmless?

Whether our meats and poultry are fresh or processed, pre-

A modern poultry farm where laying hens are permanently caged

pared in fast-food restaurants or in home kitchens, vegetarians seem to have some sound arguments for avoiding them as potential health hazards. Today a higher percentage of Americans are dying of heart attacks and cancer than ever before. These two leading killer diseases appear to be closely linked to the fats and chemicals that the meat industry has introduced into its animal products.

Lacto- and ovo-lacto-vegetarians point to surveys showing that Seventh Day Adventists who follow meatless diets have one-half the cancer rate of other Americans and only 60 percent the rate of heart disease. Vegetarians also tend to weigh less than meat eaters; the bulkiness of whole grains, fresh fruits, and other high-fiber vegetable foods is more filling than the sugars and other refined foods that usually accompany the meat eater's diet.

Other scientific studies have shown that many more people in the top meat-eating countries, like the United States, New Zealand, and Australia, get bowel cancer than do the peoples of Mexico, Central and South America, Africa, and Japan,

Enjoying a bowl of rice in Hong Kong, where most
of the harbor-dwelling population eats a rice-fish-and-vegetable diet

who eat very little meat. Yet when Japanese move to the United States and exchange their rice-fish-and-vegetable diet for a meat diet, their bowel-cancer rate begins to increase. Both a high-meat and a low-fiber diet seem to contribute to the development of bowel cancer.

Even for those of us who are not quite ready to give up meat altogether, eating less meat *and* eating what comes naturally should prove a helpful step toward better health and toward getting more flavor, freshness, variety, and food value from the food we do eat. Unprocessed foods are money savers, too, for they pass more directly from the farmer to the consumer, incurring fewer costs for packaging, storage, transportation, and advertising.

The final proof, of course, is in the eating. So our next step is to sample some recipes that show how complementary proteins and natural foods may be used in the vegetarian way.

# CHAPTER FIVE

# RECIPES FOR VEGETARIAN EATING

The idea of cramming complementary proteins into a dessert or of having a thick, protein-rich bean soup or a high-protein potato-and-cheese dish as a main course at lunch or dinner may strike a peculiar note. Among meat-eating Americans it is customary to have an animal-flesh centerpiece as the principal source of protein in a meal.

Centerpiece really is the word for it. Just think of a candelabralike crown roast of pork or lamb, a tall-standing rib roast, or a Thanksgiving turkey in all its glory.

Eating the vegetarian way is rather different. As shown by the following recipes, we can obtain delicious and healthful protein nourishment at breakfast, lunch, and dinner from *all* the courses on the menu, and even from such sweet snacks as cookies and fudge. The protein ingredients are listed at the conclusion of each recipe, showing the complementary sources provided as well as any additional protein.

All of the recipes use natural, unprocessed ingredients wherever possible. For better baking results, it is sometimes preferable to use *some* enriched white flour along with the whole-wheat flour. But the white flour should be of the unbleached variety; bleaching (which is done to increase whiteness) destroys the vitamin E in the flour.

The type of fat or oil to be used—butter, corn oil, olive oil, etc.—is indicated for each recipe and has been selected on the basis of healthfulness, wholesomeness, flavor, and suitability for that dish. When yogurt is called for, use plain yogurt, unflavored and unsweetened, made from either whole milk or

low-fat milk. Honey and dark brown sugar are the only sweet-
eners used. They are flavorful and contain traces of vitamins
and minerals, although these traces are very, very slight. No
refined white sugar is called for in any of the recipes.

Eating the vegetarian way does not imply that we must all
become plant eaters without further delay. Getting used to a
new diet takes time, and changes should be approached
gradually. Perhaps, however, this sampling of the way vegetarians eat will help to bring us back to basics and serve to re-
introduce us to the good foods of the earth.

### Metric Conversion Table

The amounts of the ingredients called for in the recipes in this book
can be converted to metric units as follows:

#### Volume

| | | |
|---|---|---|
| 1 teaspoon | = | 5 milliliters |
| 1 tablespoon | = | 15 milliliters |
| 1 fluid ounce | = | 30 milliliters |
| 1 cup | = | 0.24 liter |
| 1 pint | = | 0.47 liter |
| 1 quart | = | 0.95 liter |

(to convert liters to quarts, multiply by 1.06)

#### Weight

| | | |
|---|---|---|
| 1 ounce | = | 28 grams |
| 3½ ounces | = | 100 grams |
| 4 ounces | = | 114 grams |
| 8 ounces | = | 227 grams |
| 1 pound | = | 0.45 kilogram |
| 2.2 pounds | = | 1 kilogram |

(to convert grams to ounces, multiply by .035)

## Apple or Banana Breakfast Pancakes

¾ cup whole-wheat flour,
    unsifted
1 teaspoon baking powder
½ teaspoon baking soda
¼ teaspoon salt
½ teaspoon cinnamon
2 tablespoons butter
1 egg
½ cup milk
½ cup yogurt

1 tablespoon honey
¾ to 1 cup shredded or coarsely
    grated apple (use a tart,
    juicy variety, like Mc-
    Intosh), *or* very thinly
    sliced ripe banana, *or*
    use fresh blueberries
    in season
butter and corn oil for
    frying

In a medium-size mixing bowl, combine flour, baking powder, baking soda, salt, and cinnamon. With a pastry blender or two knives worked crisscross, cut in the butter until it is the size of small peas.

In another bowl, beat the egg, and add the milk, yogurt, and honey. Grease a large griddle or frying pan with equal parts of butter and corn oil, enough to cover the surface generously. Heat until a few drops of water bubble and dance when tossed into the pan.

Add wet ingredients to dry ingredients and stir just until blended. Add shredded apple or sliced banana. Spoon batter onto hot griddle to form rounds about 4 inches in diameter. Turn when tops are puffed and show air bubbles, and bottoms are brown. Reduce heat slightly and cook pancakes on other side until golden brown. Serve immediately, repeating until all the batter is used.

Serve *Apple or Banana Breakfast Pancakes* with honey or maple syrup. If preferred, omit fruit from pancake batter and serve bananas, berries, peaches, or other fresh fruit on top of pancakes with a little honey. Makes 10 to 12 pancakes.

*Protein Ingredients*
complementary proteins:  ¾ cup whole-wheat flour *plus* ½ cup
                             milk (grains plus milk)
additional proteins:   1 egg
                       ½ cup yogurt

## Barley-and-Garbanzo Soup

¾ cup dried, uncooked chick-peas (garbanzo beans)

¼ cup whole or coarse barley, uncooked

7 cups water

1 large onion, cut in ¼-inch dice

1 clove garlic, finely cut or put through garlic press

2 large carrots, scraped clean and cut in ¼-inch dice

2 ribs celery, scraped clean and cut in ¼-inch dice

3 to 4 celery tops with leaves, cut up

2 tablespoons fresh parsley, finely cut

2 bay leaves

2 teaspoons salt

⅛ teaspoon freshly ground black pepper

1½ teaspoons sharp-flavored mustard, dry or prepared type

1 tablespoon olive oil

1 teaspoon lemon juice

Chick-peas will cook more quickly if they are presoaked. In advance of preparing soup, place washed chick-peas in a saucepan with water to cover, bring to a boil, and simmer for 3 to 5 minutes. Remove pan from heat, cover, and let beans soak for at least 2 hours or overnight.

Drain chick-peas, discarding soak water, and place them in a 4-quart soup pot. Add barley, which has been washed in a strainer, water, onion, garlic, carrots, celery, celery tops, parsley, and bay leaves. Cover pot and bring to a boil. Skim off any foam that rises to the top, and simmer on low heat for 2½ to 3 hours, or until chick-peas are tender.

Add salt, pepper, mustard, olive oil, and lemon juice, adjusting seasoning to taste. Remove bay leaves. To give soup a thicker base, one cup of soup mixture may be whirred smooth in the blender and returned to the soup pot. Serve *Barley-and-Garbanzo Soup* with whole-grain bread or rolls or warmed whole-wheat pita bread (Middle Eastern-type "pocket" bread). If desired, add a dollop of cold yogurt to the hot soup. Makes about 6 cups, or 4 to 6 servings.

*Protein Ingredients*
complementary proteins: ¾ cup chick-peas *plus* ¼ cup barley and whole-grain bread, eaten with soup (beans plus grains)
additional protein: yogurt, if added to soup

## French-Toasted Cheese Sandwiches

8 slices whole-wheat bread
butter, slightly softened
ketchup or mustard
Cheddar, Swiss, or other
    natural (unprocessed) cheese
pickle relish, chopped green
    olives, chopped sweet onions,
    chopped red and green
    peppers

flour, whole-wheat or
    unbleached white
2 eggs
2 tablespoons milk
oil for frying (safflower, sun-
    flower, corn, or peanut)

Arrange bread slices on a large cutting board and butter surfaces. Spread ketchup or mustard on four of the slices and neatly place slices of cheese on top, not overlapping edges of bread. Top cheese with pickle relish, olives, and/or chopped onions and peppers, as desired. Sharp Cheddar cheese goes well with ketchup, pickle relish, and onions. Choose whatever combinations you prefer.

Top each cheese-covered slice with a slice of buttered bread to form 4 sandwiches. Press down firmly and cut each sandwich diagonally to form 2 triangles. Sprinkle a little flour on cutting board and lightly coat all sides of triangles.

In a wide, shallow bowl, beat eggs and milk. To a 10-inch skillet add oil just to cover the bottom, and heat to near sizzling. Carefully dip each sandwich triangle into egg mixture, covering edges and both sides completely, and arrange in skillet.

When triangles are golden-brown on bottom, turn with a broad spatula. Lower heat slightly and fry sandwiches on other side until bread is golden-brown and cheese is melted. Remove and place on paper toweling to drain off excess oil.

Serve *French-Toasted Cheese Sandwiches* hot and eat them with a knife and fork. Crisp, freshly made cole slaw is a good accompaniment. Makes 4 whole sandwiches.

*Protein Ingredients*
complementary proteins: 8 slices whole-wheat bread *plus* cheese
(grains plus dairy products)
additional proteins: 2 eggs
2 tablespoons milk

### Potato-Cheese-and-Mushroom Bake

6 medium-large potatoes, pared
    and cut in large slices,
    3/8-inch thick
3 tablespoons butter
1 1/2 cups milk
4 tablespoons unbleached
    white flour
1 teaspoon salt
1/8 teaspoon white pepper
1 small clove garlic, put
    through garlic press

1 egg
1 1/2 cups coarsely grated cheese
    (Muenster or similar mild-
    flavored variety)
1 cup sliced fresh mushrooms
    that have been lightly
    browned in a small amount
    of hot butter
2 tablespoons freshly grated
    Parmesan cheese

Cook potatoes in boiling water to which 2 teaspoons of salt have been added for about 15 minutes, or until slices are just tender. Pour off water and put potatoes back on heating unit (with heat turned off), shaking saucepan very gently so that potatoes dry thoroughly. Transfer potatoes to a bowl, being careful not to break the slices, and set aside. Set oven to heat to 350 degrees Fahrenheit.

In saucepan in which potatoes cooked, melt the butter. In a small bowl, add the flour to about half the milk, and beat with a wire whisk until mixture is perfectly smooth. Add remaining milk, beat smooth, and add all of the milk-and-flour mixture to the butter in the saucepan. Cook over medium-high heat until the mixture has thickened, beating frequently with whisk to keep lumps from forming. Add salt, pepper, and garlic.

In a medium-size bowl, beat the egg. Slowly add the hot, thickened milk mixture to the egg, beating constantly with wire whisk. Lightly butter an 8 x 8 x 2 baking dish. Arrange half of the potato slices on the bottom. Sprinkle with half the coarsely grated Muenster cheese, half the mushrooms, and half the thickened milk sauce. Repeat, using up the remainder of these ingredients. Spread the sauce evenly to cover the contents of the baking dish, and sprinkle with the grated Parmesan cheese.

Bake at 350 degrees for 40 minutes, or until top is puffy and browned. Serve *Potato-Cheese-and-Mushroom Bake* directly from baking dish, along with a leafy green salad. Makes about 6 servings.

*Protein Ingredients*
complementary proteins:  6 potatoes *plus* 1½ cups milk and 1½
                         cups grated cheese (potatoes plus
                         dairy products)
additional proteins:  1 egg
                      1 cup sliced mushrooms

## Old-Fashioned Baked Beans

1 pound pea beans (also called        2½ teaspoons salt
  navy beans), about 2 cups            1 teaspoon dry English
1 medium-size onion, cut in               mustard, or other sharp-
  ¼-inch dice                             flavored type
½ cup ketchup                          bean liquor (1½ to 2 cups)
⅓ cup molasses

Wash beans in a strainer, pick over, and place in a large bowl.
Add cold water to at least 2 inches above the beans, and let stand
overnight in a cool place. Next day put beans and soak water into
a 4-quart pot. Add water, if necessary, to come to 1 inch above
beans. Cover, bring to a boil, skim off white froth that comes to
the top, lower heat and simmer covered for about 45 minutes, or
until beans are just beginning to get tender.

Set oven at 300 degrees Fahrenheit. Drain beans, being sure
to keep the water, or bean liquor, in which they cooked. Combine
onion, ketchup, molasses, salt, and mustard, and gently mix
through the drained beans. Grease a 2-quart bean pot or casserole
dish with butter or oil. Add beans. Bake, covered, for 3 hours at
300 degrees, adding reserved bean liquor—¼ to ½ cup at a time—
when beans begin to look dry. Mixture should be fairly loose and
bubbly as beans bake. After 3 hours, remove cover from bean pot
and bake ½ hour longer.

Serve *Old-Fashioned Baked Beans* with a tangy cole slaw
and cornbread such as *Carrot Corn Muffins*. Makes 6 to 8 servings.

*Protein Ingredients*
complementary proteins:  baked beans *plus* corn muffins (beans
                         plus corn)
additional proteins:  1 egg (in corn muffins)
                      1 cup milk (in corn muffins)

## Carrot Corn Muffins

1 cup yellow cornmeal (containing the germ)
½ cup whole-wheat flour, unsifted
½ cup unbleached white flour (not necessary to sift)
2½ teaspoons baking powder
1 teaspoon salt

1 egg
¼ cup corn oil
3 tablespoons honey
1 cup milk
½ cup shredded raw carrot
2 teaspoons finely grated raw onion (optional)

In a medium-large mixing bowl, combine the cornmeal, whole-wheat flour, white flour, baking powder, and salt. In another bowl, beat the egg, and then beat in the oil, honey, and milk.

Set oven at 425 degrees Fahrenheit. While oven is heating, shred the carrot and grate the onion. Prepare one or two muffin tins, brushing the insides of the muffin cups well with a little additional corn oil. Add the wet ingredients to the dry ingredients, mixing just enough to moisten and blend. Do not beat. Add carrot and onion.

Fill muffin cups about two-thirds full with batter. Bake at 425 degrees for 20 minutes or until muffins are golden-brown and tops spring back to the touch. Remove from tins at once, running a sharp knife around the edges to loosen the muffins. Serve *Carrot Corn Muffins* warm from oven, or reheated, with butter. Makes 12 large or 16 medium-size muffins.

*Protein Ingredients*
complementary proteins: cornmeal *plus* beans, when muffins are
            served with baked beans, bean soups,
            bean salads, or other bean dishes
additional proteins:  1 egg
            1 cup milk

## Whole-Wheat Pizzas

12 whole-wheat, Middle Eastern-type pita bread rounds (small size, about 4 inches in diameter)
olive oil

1½ cups tomato sauce for pizzas (see recipe below)
½ pound mozzarella cheese, coarsely shredded or thinly sliced

sliced fresh mushrooms, lightly browned in a little hot butter, *or* sweet red pepper strips lightly fried in a little olive oil, *or* ripe black olives, cut up

¾ cup freshly grated Parmesan cheese
dried oregano, freshly ground black pepper, garlic powder (optional)

*Tomato Sauce for Pizzas*

2 tablespoons olive oil
1 medium-large onion, cut in ¼-inch dice
1 clove garlic, put through garlic press
1 1-pound, 12-ounce can crushed concentrated tomatoes *or* whole tomatoes in thick tomato puree
1½ teaspoons salt

⅛ teaspoon freshly ground black pepper
½ teaspoon dried oregano
½ teaspoon dried basil
1 tablespoon finely cut fresh parsley *or* 1 teaspoon dried parsley
1 bay leaf
1 teaspoon honey

Prepare tomato sauce in advance. In a deep 10-inch skillet, heat the olive oil. Add onion and garlic and cook until onion is limp. Add tomatoes and all remaining ingredients. If using whole tomatoes, cut them into small pieces. If using canned tomatoes that are packed in a thin liquid, add 3 to 4 tablespoons of canned tomato paste. Simmer sauce, uncovered, over low heat for 1 to 1½ hours or until thickened. Stir frequently. Cool and refrigerate. Makes about 3 cups. Unused sauce can be stored in freezer for long keeping.

To prepare pizzas, set oven at 400 degrees Fahrenheit. Brush the hollow, or inward-curving, sides of the pita rounds with a little olive oil. (Pita breads can also be split into two thin rounds if very thin-crusted pizzas are wanted. In that case, you will need only 6 pita bread rounds for recipe.)

Place the 12 oiled bread rounds on a large, flat baking pan and bake 5 to 10 minutes, or until bread is lightly crisped. Remove from oven and spread each round with tomato sauce, cover with shredded mozzarella cheese, and sprinkle with mushrooms, sweet peppers, or black olives, alone or in any combination desired. Top each pizza with about 1 tablespoon of grated Parmesan cheese and a little oregano and/or black pepper, if desired.

Return pizzas to oven and bake 15 minutes, or until cheese is melted and bubbly. Serve immediately, sprinkled with a little garlic powder, if desired. Serve *Whole-Wheat Pizzas* with raw vegetables that can be eaten with the fingers or with a crisp, mixed salad. Makes 4 to 6 servings.

**Note:** If whole-wheat pita bread is unobtainable, 6 English muffins, split in half, can be used instead. To increase protein value, sprinkle ¼ teaspoon of wheat germ on each muffin half after brushing with olive oil.

*Protein Ingredients*
complementary proteins:  whole-wheat bread *plus* ½ pound mozzarella cheese and ¾ cup Parmesan cheese (grains plus dairy products)
additional protein: mushrooms, if used

## Brown-Rice-and-Date Pudding

½ cup brown rice, washed in a strainer and drained
4 cups milk (1 quart)
2 tablespoons butter

¼ cup dark brown sugar, firmly packed
½ teaspoon cinnamon
1 tablespoon grated orange rind
½ cup cut-up dates

Set oven to heat to 300 degrees Fahrenheit. Lightly butter a 2-quart baking dish. Put in rice, milk, butter, the brown sugar that has been blended with the cinnamon and orange rind, and the dates.

Bake uncovered at 300 degrees for 2½ hours, stirring pudding 3 to 4 times during the baking period so that ingredients will be evenly distributed. Serve *Brown-Rice-and-Date Pudding* warm, with a dollop of cold yogurt, or serve it chilled. Makes 6 servings.

*Protein Ingredients*
complementary proteins:  ½ cup brown rice *plus* 4 cups milk (grains plus milk)
additional protein: yogurt, if eaten with pudding

## Cranberry-Orange Nut Bread

1 cup unbleached white flour, sifted
1½ teaspoons baking powder
½ teaspoon baking soda
¼ teaspoon salt
1 cup whole-wheat flour, unsifted
1 cup dark brown sugar, firmly packed
⅓ cup instant nonfat milk powder
¼ cup butter (⅛ pound, or ½ stick)
1 egg
1 tablespoon grated orange rind
1 cup orange juice
½ cup coarsely chopped walnuts
1 cup fresh cranberries, washed and cut in halves or thirds with a small, serrated knife

Have cranberries ready. Grease a 9 x 5 x 3 loaf pan with a little butter or oil, and set oven at 350 degrees Fahrenheit.

Combine sifted white flour, baking powder, baking soda, and salt, and sift into a large mixing bowl. Add whole-wheat flour, brown sugar, and milk powder. Add the ¼ cup butter in chunks, and cut in with a pastry blender or with two knives worked crisscross fashion until the mixture has the texture of coarse crumbs.

In a medium-small mixing bowl, beat egg, add grated orange rind, and orange juice. Add this mixture to the dry ingredients in the large mixing bowl, and stir with a wooden spoon until just moistened and blended. Add walnuts and cranberries. Spoon into loaf pan.

Bake at 350 degrees for one hour or until the center of the bread springs back to the touch and the edges stand away slightly from the sides of the baking pan. A cake tester inserted in the center of the bread should come out dry.

Remove bread from oven and let cool on a rack for 10 minutes. Loosen edges with a sharp knife and slip bread upside down onto another rack. Turn right side up. Slice when thoroughly cool.

*Cranberry-Orange Nut Bread* should be tightly wrapped and stored in a cool, dry place, or it may be stored in the freezer. Makes one loaf.

*Protein Ingredients*
complementary proteins: 2 cups flour *plus* ⅓ cup milk powder (grains plus milk)
additional proteins:    1 egg
                        ½ cup walnuts

## *Dream Bar Cookies*

*Cookie Base*

1 cup whole-wheat flour, unsifted

¼ cup dark brown sugar, firmly packed

¼ pound butter (1 stick)

Set oven at 350 degrees Fahrenheit. In a medium-large mixing bowl, combine flour and brown sugar. Add butter in chunks and cut it in with a pastry blender or two knives worked crisscross fashion until the mixture is moist and crumbly and the butter is well distributed throughout. Lightly butter an 8 x 8 x 2 or 9 x 9 x 2 baking pan and firmly pat mixture into bottom of pan in an even layer. Bake for 12 minutes at 350 degrees.

*Topping Mixture for Cookies*

2 eggs

⅓ cup honey

½ teaspoon vanilla extract

¼ cup whole-wheat flour, unsifted

½ teaspoon baking powder

¼ teaspoon salt

½ cup chocolate chips or carob chips (Carob is a naturally sweet, cocoalike product made from a dried seed pod called St. John's Bread.)

½ cup sunflower seeds

⅓ cup chopped roasted peanuts (without salt or added fat)

While cookie base is baking, prepare topping. In a medium-large mixing bowl, beat eggs with a wire whisk. Beat in honey. Add vanilla. Combine the ¼ cup of flour with the baking powder and salt. Add to egg mixture and mix until just blended. Add chocolate or carob chips, sunflower seeds, and peanuts. Pour evenly over baked cookie base, and return to oven to bake 25 minutes longer at 350 degrees. When *Dream Bar Cookies* are thoroughly cooled, cut contents of pan into 6 strips in one direction and 4 in the other. Makes 24 bars.

*Protein Ingredients*

complementary proteins:  ½ cup sunflower seeds *plus* ⅓ cup peanuts (seeds plus legumes)

additional protein: 2 eggs

## Peanut-Butter Fudge

½ cup chunk-style peanut butter (unsweetened, unhy-drogenated type is best)
½ cup honey
½ cup instant nonfat milk powder

3 tablespoons dry cocoa (3 tablespoons carob powder may be used instead, but fudge will be sweeter and less chocolaty)
4 tablespoons dark raisins
⅔ cup finely chopped walnuts

In a medium-small mixing bowl, combine peanut butter, honey, milk powder, and cocoa. Work with the back of a spoon to blend. Add raisins and blend thoroughly.

With your fingers, roll fudge into balls about ¾ of an inch in diameter. Roll each ball in finely chopped walnuts so that it is well coated. Store *Peanut-Butter Fudge* in refrigerator and serve chilled or at room temperature. Makes about 40 pieces.

*Protein Ingredients*
complementary proteins:  ½ cup peanut butter *plus* ½ cup milk powder (peanuts plus milk)
additional protein: ⅔ cup walnuts

# BIBLIOGRAPHY

Barkas, Janet. *The Vegetable Passion.* New York: Charles Scribner's
   Sons, 1975.
DeVore, Sally and White, Thelma. *The Appetites of Man.* New York:
   Anchor/Doubleday, 1978.
Doyle, Rodger P. and Redding, James L. *The Complete Food Hand-*
   *book.* New York: Grove Press, 1978.
Doyle, Rodger. *The Vegetarian Handbook: A Guide to Vegetarian*
   *Nutrition.* New York: Crown, 1979.
Ewald, Ellen Buchman. *Recipes for a Small Planet.* New York: Ballan-
   tine, 1973.
Ford, Barbara. *Future Food: Alternate Protein for the Year 2000.* New
   York: William Morrow, 1978.
Lappé, Frances Moore. *Diet for a Small Planet.* New York: Ballantine,
   1975.
Stare, Frederick J. and McWilliams, Margaret. *Living Nutrition.* New
   York: John Wiley & Sons, 1977.
Wellford, Harrison. *Sowing the Wind: A Report from Ralph Nader's*
   *Center for Study of Responsive Law on Food Safety and the*
   *Chemical Harvest.* New York: Grossman, 1972.

# INDEX

* indicates illustration
*italics indicate recipe*

## ABOUT THE AUTHOR

Lila Perl was born in New York City, and she graduated from Brooklyn College with a B.A. degree, having majored in food-science education and minored in English. In addition, she has taken graduate work at Teachers College, Columbia University, and at the School of Education, New York University. She is the author of thirty books, both fiction and nonfiction, mainly for young people. Her interest in Americana and in foreign cultures is reflected in *America Goes to the Fair* and in her many books about African and Latin American nations. Her knowledge of foods and nutrition led to the writing of *The Global Food Shortage*, which was published in 1976. Miss Perl is married to a writer, Charles Yerkow, and lives in Beechhurst, New York.